BRIDGE QUIZ

Every bridge player loves to read about Bridge hands, to see where "South" brought off a coup or perhaps where somebody "chucked". When the hands are good, as this collection undoubtedly is, then there is real enjoyment for the keen student.

These hands will instruct the beginner, enlarge the horizon of the advanced player and challenge the honesty of the expert. He will face the question, "Would I have found the right bid or play?"

BRIDGE QUIZ

by

Ben Cohen

FOYLES HANDBOOKS
LONDON

ISBN 0 7071 0577 3

Published in Great Britain by
W. & G. Foyle Ltd.,
125 Charing Cross Road,
London, WC2H 0EB

Printed and bound in Great Britain by
REDWOOD BURN LIMITED
Trowbridge & Esher

FOREWORD

THE TWENTIETH CENTURY has given us the Quiz. It is the impersonal monitor, the silent teacher that asks whether we have done our homework properly. We may seek to evade the impositions of a human teacher, but the demands of the Quiz are not to be denied, for it asks us to be honest with ourselves.

No one, then, could deny the merits of a Quiz for the Bridge player. When that Quiz is compiled by Ben Cohen it is bound to be good, for Mr. Cohen has been known for many years as an international Bridge player, as an analyst and writer, and as the first to set forth the principles of the Acol system in print.

The hands are the result of careful selection and illustrate interesting and instructive points of bidding and play. You will learn not only what is the right bid, but you will be shown what bids you must avoid. You are not given a mere set of rules to commit to memory, but you are led to see the logic behind each sequence in the bidding. In the play of the cards, too, the clear exposition of the salient points of the hand cannot fail to give you a greater grasp of how to handle the dummy play, or conduct the defence with the confidence born of understanding.

I have enjoyed *Bridge Quiz* – I have found it stimulating and refreshing. I can confidently recommend it to the Bridge player, whether he is a Novice, Expert or steady Palooka!

E. P. C. COTTER

QUESTION 1

The auction proceeds:

West	North	East	South
No bid	1♠	2♡	?

What should you, South, bid on:

♠J 9 7 2; ♡A Q 10 8; ◇K 5 3; ♣10 6

QUESTION 2

You deal yourself: ♠K 10 9 6 4
♡A K Q 10 5
◇J 5 4
♣—

What do you bid?

QUESTION 3

You deal yourself: ♠A Q 7 2
♡A J 4 2
◇A 5 3
♣A 7

What do you bid?

QUESTION 4

The auction proceeds:

South	West	North	East
1◇	No bid	1♡	1♠

What should you, South, bid on:

♠Q 4   ♡J 3   ◇A Q J 4 2   ♣K 8 5 3

ANSWER 1: Three Spades

Why: First of all, you thought of doubling with all those good heart honours over the bidder. Suppose you *do* make 4 tricks in hearts (and West may easily hold ♡J, which will cut you down to 3 tricks); suppose you even make ◇K – how many spade tricks do you think you will make? With four cards in partner's suit, you should always look for your own contract before you double opponents. You would have bid 3♠ without the butt-in of hearts; bid it despite!

ANSWER 2: One Spade

Why: With two biddable suits of equal length (5 cards and more) and adjacent rank (that is, spades and hearts; hearts and diamonds; diamonds and clubs), bid the higher-ranking first. This is to make the bidding easy and economical. If you open 1♡ (either because you feel it is the stronger suit or because you want to score 100 for honours) and partner responds 2♣, you will have to bid 2♠. Now, if he has a bad hand with a singleton spade and three little hearts, he will have to *raise* the contract to put you back to your first suit.

ANSWER 3: One Heart

Why: To begin with, you are too good for 1NT, so you must compromise with one of a suit bid. You might think that you should open with 1♠ – the higher-ranking suit. You don't because you are hoping to play this hand in no-trumps – *not* because you have 150 for aces, but because you have no predominant suit. But you do not want to miss a heart or spade contract if one be available. You open 1♡ so that partner can raise you if he has heart support, and can overbid with spades if he has a spade suit. If you open 1♠, he may not be able to overbid in hearts.

ANSWER 4: No Bid

Why: When you opened 1◇, and partner responded 1♡, you were obliged to find another bid – either 2◇, 2♣ or 1NT. Now East has bid 1♠, you cannot bid 1NT because you have no spade stop; you cannot raise partner because you have only two cards in hearts; and because you are minimum, you should welcome the opportunity of passing. In fact, you should thank East politely for enabling you to tell North that you had an opening bid but no more!

QUESTION 5

The auction proceeds:

South	West	North	East
1♠	No bid	2♡	No bid

What should you, South, bid on:

    ♠A K J 6 3   ♡K J 9 5 2   ◇ –   ♣A 9 2

QUESTION 6

East deals and bids 4♡. What should you, South, bid on:

    ♠A 4
    ♡ –
    ◇A J 10 6 3 2
    ♣K Q J 10 7

QUESTION 7

You deal and bid 1♠ and partner jumps to 4♠ – a bid of some, though not great, strength. What further bid, if any, do you make on these cards?

    ♠A J 8 6 4   ♡ –   ◇K Q 9 7 2   ♣A K 3

QUESTION 8

You play a strong no-trump. What do you bid on:

    ♠K 7   ♡A J 10 4   ◇A Q 10   ♣A J 10 6

ANSWER 5: Four Clubs

Why: The one thing for which you could not hope when you opened 1♠ was that partner was going to respond in hearts. This bid has improved your hand enormously, and you have almost the certainty of slam. But rather than bid 6♡ right away, you make a bid which enables you to explore at leisure. Now although you have no third genuine suit you still bid 4♣. This will enable you to discover whether to play in 6♡ or 7♡ – or, perhaps, you will stop in 5♡.

ANSWER 6: Four No-trumps

Why: Merely to double 4♡ would announce you hoped to play against that contract and defeat it. In fact, what you want is to learn which is partner's longest (and least bad) suit. Over a bid of 1♡, you would have bid 2♡, compelling partner to speak; but when the opening is 4♡, you cannot double (because that would be for business, not take-out) and you cannot bid 5♡ or you would compel partner to bid 6♣ or 6◇. So you use 4NT as a take-out double, requesting partner to bid his *best* minor suit.

ANSWER 7: Five Clubs

Why: Because the hand is worth an effort of some sort; and you are anxious to know which ace (if any) responder holds. If he has the ace of diamonds, you will be in seven; if the ace of hearts (on which you can shed your losing club), in six; if no ace, you will stop comfortably in five.

ANSWER 8: One Club

Why: The "strong" no-trump should never count more than 17–18 points; here, you have 19 points – and three tens as plus values. This is too much for 1NT – partner, with five, six or seven, will pass without giving his cards a second look: and rightly so. But this is a hand on which any response will enable you to rebid 3NT. You bid 1♣ rather than 1♡ to make it as easy as possible for him to respond. Even if he replies 1♡, you will still bid 3NT (not 4♡ or 3◇) to show the balanced nature of your hand.

QUESTION 9

You respond 1♡ to your partner's opening 1♣; over his rebid of 2♣ you try 2♠. Partner stolidly repeats his suit: 3♣. What do you say now on:

    ♠A Q 10 7   ♡A J 9 7 4   ◇J 3 2   ♣4

QUESTION 10

The dealer, on your right, bids 1♠. What do you bid on:

    ♠ –   ♡K Q J 10 9 7 6   ◇8 7   ♣A Q 5 4

QUESTION 11

Your partner, North, at game to you, opens 1♡; East, not vulnerable, bids 1♠. What action do you, South, take on:

    ♠K J 10 8 7   ♡K 10 9 4   ◇A 3   ♣K 8

QUESTION 12

Your vulnerable partner opens the bidding with 1NT (15–17 points). What do you bid on:

    ♠K J 9 5 3 2   ♡A J 8 7   ◇7   ♣8 2

ANSWER 9: No Bid

Why: Because it is clear that partner has opened on a long suit of clubs and very little else. He certainly has no effective double stop in diamonds; it is improbable he has absolutely solid clubs: so no-trumps is "out". You have done full justice to your hand by reversing in response – and partner has shown no enthusiasm for either of your major suits. If you have nothing sensible to say, hold your peace. Opener's hand was:

♠J 3　　♡10 3　　♢K 8 4　　♣A K J 10 8 3

– just enough for nine tricks with clubs as trumps.

ANSWER 10: Four Hearts

Why: A cardinal rule of bridge is this: Never ask a partner to do for you what you can do for yourself! Another cardinal rule is: When pre-empting, pre-empt as high as you possibly can. The bid of 4♡ fulfils both these rules. For one thing, you reckon about eight tricks in hand – six hearts and two clubs. It is reasonable to credit partner with about 1½ tricks: so you have a fine chance for game. Moreover, you will make it much more difficult for opponents to compete.

ANSWER 11: Three Diamonds

Why: You are too good for 4♡ direct with all your outside strength; you are also – and this is a surprise – unsuitable for a double . . *because you have four of partner's suit.* You are certain of game – but you may also be too good for it. You therefore make a "phoney" force in a lower-ranking suit, and you choose the one where you have a control. Your next bid will be determined by opener's rebid: over 3♡ you will simply bid 4♡; over 4♢ or 4♣, you will still bid no more than 4♡. But over 3NT, you will bid . . . 4♠! For this means that the spade bid was psychic and partner has an honour in the suit.

ANSWER 12: Two Clubs(!)

Why: This bid, over 1NT, is conventional, asking opener to bid any four-card major suit. If he bids 2♠ or 2♡, you will raise him direct to game in whichever suit he bids. If he has no four-card major, he will give the conventional reply of 2♢. Now you will simply bid 4♠ (not 3♠, which, after the 2♣ bid, is only invitational but a direct game bid. You have no slam hopes on your cards – and, unless opener has four hearts, you do not want the red major as a trump suit; so you bid, without further exploration, what you expect to make.

QUESTION 13

At Game All, partner opens 1♢; you reply 1♡; partner raises to 3♡. What action do you take on:

    ♠A 4 3 2   ♡A 6 4 2   ♢A   ♣A 4 3 2

QUESTION 14

At 60 up, your partner opens 1♣. What response do you make on:

    ♠A J 3   ♡Q J 4 2   ♢K 10 9   ♣K 8 5

QUESTION 15

You deal yourself: ♠8 7 6 4 2
                      ♡A
                      ♢A J 10
                      ♣A K Q 3

What opening bid do you make?

QUESTION 16

You, West, are in 4♠ on these two hands. North opened 1NT (15–17) and South bid hearts. North cashes ♣K and leads a heart. How should you play?

♠A Q 10 7 4	♠8 3 2
♡A	♡6 5 2
♢8 7 6 5 4 3	♢A 9 2
♣3	♣Q J 10 8

ANSWER 13: Four No-trumps

Why: Because opener, although aceless, is very good and you have an absolute maximum for a one-bid, including all four first-round controls. He has opened vulnerable with 1◇ and he holds four good hearts by his immediate raise. Over 4NT he will, of course, sign-off; but you will repeat with 5NT, announcing your four aces. Now he can judge whether to bid six or seven – and in which denomination: hearts, diamonds or no-trumps. Once he has bid 3♡, the *only* question in your mind should have been "Grand slam or small?"

ANSWER 14: Two No-trumps

Why: Because you are too good not to make some sort of slam try; yet you are not good enough to make a direct forcing take-out. Some players will make an underbid of 1NT in the hope that opponents will compete. With 14 points facing an opening bid, the trap of 1NT is much more likely to trap you than them: for the once you catch them for 1,100, you will miss a slam three times. Partner, hearing you overbid the game but failing to make a forcing take-out, will read you for a comfortable 3NT bid (13–14 points – which is what you have). On a mere 11 points, you would simply bid 1NT for an easy rubber.

ANSWER 15: One Club!

Why: Because you do not want, on so good a hand, to be compelled to back-pedal furiously over any response partner may make because you are afraid of your own suit. Put a single top-honour (A, K or Q) at the top of the spades instead of the 8, and you would bid a spade without fear or reproach. You will lose nothing by suppressing so weak a suit as five to the nothing: it is the sort of suit which, if bid at all, should be relegated to a secondary bid in any case.

ANSWER 16:

Cross to ◇A and finesse ♠10. On the second round of diamonds, throw dummy's ◇9.
Why: Because on his 1NT it is most probable than North holds ♠K but may not hold ♠J. Moreover, it is essential to unblock the diamonds so that you can run the long cards in your own hand. When you lose to ♠K, you will have to trump a heart. Now two rounds of trumps must be drawn and a diamond played. Even if the diamonds drop 2–2, another heart lead will take the last spade from your hand – and you will never be able to enjoy your long suit if you leave ◇9 in dummy. The "Curse of Scotland" will prove the Curse of West!

QUESTION 17

North opens 1◊ and East doubles; you, West, bid 2♡ and East goes direct to 6♡ – no bad shot. South doubles and you redouble. North leads ♣K. How do you plan the play?

West	East
♠4	♠K J 8 5 4
♡K Q J 4 2	♡A 10 8 6 5
◊10 3	◊A Q 7
♣A 9 8 7 6	♣–

QUESTION 18

You sit East and you are defending against 4♠ by South. West, who bid diamonds, leads ♣2, which you assume to be a singleton. You win with ♣A. What card do you return from:

♠7 4   ♡A 10 6 4   ◊Q 5 2   ♣A 9 7 3

QUESTION 19

You sit West and you are defending against 4♠. Both North and South have bid diamonds during the auction. What do you lead from:

♠A 5   ♡K 8 4   ◊9 7 5 3 2   ♣A 5 3

ANSWER 17:

Ruff the club small in dummy; lead a low heart to hand; ruff another club small and lead a third heart to hand. Ruff a club high.

Why: Because, on the double, it is clear that South is likely to hold (*a*) three trumps and (*b*) ♠A. North has opened on a minor two-suiter. He has not, however, five or six clubs, or he would probably have shown them over your 2♡ bid. You must not be premature in drawing trumps and you must husband prudently your high trump in dummy for a late (not an early) ruff. A careful count of tricks should show you twelve: for if South holds ♢K and ♠A, the contract is surely down – and North must have been psychic.

ANSWER 18: The Nine of Clubs

Why: Because you want West to lead a heart after he has ruffed the club, in order that you may get in at once to give him another ruff. This is called a "suit-preference" signal. It works as follows: exclude the suit led (partner cannot lead it; he had a singleton); exclude trumps. Now, of the other two suits a high card requests the lead of the higher-ranking, a low card the lead of the lower-ranking. West led clubs and spades are trumps. You want a heart return – higher-ranking than diamonds – so lead a high club back. With ♢A you would return ♣3.

ANSWER 19: The Two of Diamonds

Why: It is very probable that East is void in diamonds; it is certain he has only one diamond. You wish to give him a ruff and lead the suit. You are certain to enter at once (with ♠A) even if he has only a singleton and not a void. You lead ♢2 (not ♢9 as top of nothing or ♢3 as fourth-best) because you want him to return a club to obtain a second ruff. This is the suit-preference signal—which calls upon the partner (*a*) to discount the suit led and the trump suit; and (*b*) to choose between the remaining two suits. A high card calls for the higher-ranking of these remaining suits, a low card for the lower-ranking.

QUESTION 20

You are West and lead ♣K against South's contract of 4♡. East follows with ♣10. What do you lead next when your hand and dummy's are:

North
♠K J
♡Q 8 6 2
◇A 4 2
♣J 7 5 3

West
♠7 5 3
♡5 4
◇K 8 5 3
♣A K 8 6

QUESTION 21

You are West, defending against South's 4♠. You lead ♣K and East plays ♣J. What is your next lead when your hand and dummy's are:

North
♠J 8 7 4
♡Q 6 3
◇A K J 5 4
♣6

West
♠5 3
♡J 5 2
◇Q 9 6
♣A K 10 4 3

QUESTION 22

You are West, defending against 6♠ after the bidding: 4♠ by South, 6♠ by North. You lead ♣K and East drops ♣J. What do you lead to Trick 2 when your hand and dummy's are:

North
♠Q J
♡A K J 7 5
◇A K 10 8 6
♣5

West
♠8
♡Q 7 5 3
◇J 8 6
♣A K 8 4 2

ANSWER 20: The Ace of Clubs

Why: After the previous questions in this Quiz, you may be betrayed into thinking that East is anxious, *via* a suit-preference signal, for a switch to spades. He is nothing of the kind! He is simply telling you to continue clubs—either he has ♣Q 10 9 2 and wants to force South to ruff; or he has ♣10 2 and wants to ruff himself. He may have ♣Q 10 bare – in which case he will still come to a ruff. If he had ♣Q 10 2 and ♠A Q, he should refrain from playing high; he should be anxious for you to switch – and, by playing ♣2, would discourage a club continuation. It would not be very difficult for you to try the spade. Suit-preference must not be over-done; the normal signals of encouragement and discouragement are still made; suit-preference occurs only when there is no ambiguity.

ANSWER 21: The Knave of Hearts

Why: Because East is clearly screaming for a switch. It is highly improbable that South holds six clubs and has not bid them. East is making it very clear to you that he has heart tricks; he may even have ♡A K 10. If East has no more than four cards in the suit, you will defeat the contract before South can get in. East is employing the suit-preference signal; playing a high card for the higher-ranking suit, after discounting the suit led and trumps.

ANSWER 22: The Ace of Clubs

Why: It is inconceivable that East has a singleton in clubs or void in hearts after such bidding. This is a normal encouraging card; nay, more, it is a scream to tell you to continue with clubs. Now, why should East want you to give dummy a ruff and, perhaps, establish South's ♣Q? Only because he wants dummy to be compelled to ruff. East actually held ♠K 10 in a valueless hand and, by making dummy ruff at Trick 2, established the setting trick. It is only when there is, and can be, no ambiguity at all that suit-preference signals should be made.

QUESTION 23

You are on lead against South's 3NT. You start off, normally, with
♠K and follow with ♠J. Dummy holds three small cards in spades
and partner follows twice. What card do you lead to Trick 3 from:

    ♠K Q J 5 2   ♡A 4   ◇10 6 4   ♣9 7 2

QUESTION 24

Partner bids 1♠; what do you respond on:

    ♠A 9 5 3   ♡4   ◇K J 10 7 5   ♣A J 7

QUESTION 25

Partner, North, bids 3◇; East bids 3NT (asking for a take-out from
West); what do you, South, bid on:

    ♠J 4 3 2   ♡5 3   ◇K J 9 5 4 2   ♣10

ANSWER 23: The Queen of Spades

Why: Because you want to show partner how to put you back to cash your good spades. You use the suit-preference signal – playing the highest card for the highest-ranking suit. In no-trumps, you can sometimes pin-point the suit in which you hold your entry; not only between two, but even between three suits. There is no trump suit to discount, but only the suit led. If you held ♣A instead of ♡A, you would lead ♠2 to Trick 3, asking for the lowest-ranking suit; and if you held ♢A, you would lead ♠5 – the middle card to ask for the middle suit.

ANSWER 24: Two Diamonds

Why: Because you are too good for 3♠; too good for 4♠; and not quite good enough for a forcing take-out of 3♢. Over any rebid, you will go to 4♠ – and partner will now know that you are well worth 4♠. If he bids hearts, raises diamonds or bids clubs, he will recognize that you have made a "delayed game raise" – which is stronger than anything short of a direct jump take-out If he rebids a mere 2♠, he will not know you are quite so good . . . but that will not matter because, if he is minimum, there will be no slam anyway!

ANSWER 25: Five (or even six!) Diamonds

Why: Because North has clearly said he has virtually no defence by opening with a pre-emptive bid; you can see from your own cards that you have no defence – North must hold at least six, and possibly seven cards in diamonds, so you have not even ♢A to cash. In these circumstances, it is sure that East-West have a slam. By bidding to your outside limit at once, you will make them guess which slam to bid (or compel them to double you for an inferior result). In the event, when this hand occurred, West guessed wrong and bid 6♠. He went one down with 7♡ cold – all because South bounced to 6♢.

QUESTION 26

You deal and bid 1♠; partner forces with 3♣; what do you rebid when you hold:

♠A K Q J 5 3   ♡K 4 2   ◇K 4 3   ♣7

QUESTION 27

Partner deals and bids 1NT (15–17 points). What do you respond on:

♠7   ♡J 8 4   ◇8 7 3   ♣A K J 10 6 3

QUESTION 28

Partner deals and bids 1NT (15—17 points). What do you respond on:

♠7   ♡J 10 9 3   ◇7 3   ♣A K 10 6 3

QUESTION 29

Partner deals and bids 1NT (15–17 points). What do you respond on:

♠7   ♡J 8 4   ◇7 3   ♣Q J 10 8 6 4 2

ANSWER 26: Four Spades

Why: Because, when a forcing situation is in being, there is no normal need to jump; in fact, you should go slowly, to explore and avail yourself of every inch of bidding-space. If you *do* jump, you do it with a purpose – to tell partner that you have an absolutely solid suit, self-sustaining, with no loser (the risk of an adverse five-to-the-ten may be accepted), and at least six cards long. The bid must not be made with a five-card suit, even if it consists of 150 honours. This type of jump-bid will facilitate slam-bidding immeasurably.

ANSWER 27: Three No-trumps

Why: It is pointless to show your club suit. Your hand should be worth 5½–6½ tricks to opener; and a 15-count should produce three tricks. Do not be deterred by the singleton spade. You can have no ambition to make eleven tricks with these cards – and you should never sacrifice a probable game merely to score 100 honours. What will happen, you may ask, if opener does not hold ♣Q or if opponents run five spades at once? In the latter case you will, and in the former you may, go down. The outside risk of failure should not prevent you from making your proper bid.

ANSWER 28: Two Clubs

Why: Because it is possible that opener holds a four-card heart suit, which he should bid in response to this request for a four-card major. Two clubs over partner's 1NT is a strictly conventional bid – and the mere fact that you have a huge club suit is quite irrelevant. If opener does not bid 2♡, but replies 2♠ or 2◇ – the latter denying any four-card major, a bid equally conventional as your 2♣ – you will simply go to 3NT. This is a cost-nothing inquiry which may well lead to a contract of 4♡, safer than 3NT.

ANSWER 29: Two Clubs

Why: Because, although opener will (quite correctly) take this as an inquiry for a four-card major, and will reply either with 2♡ or 2♠ (or 2◇ if he has no four-card major suit), you will swiftly disillusion him by repeating your clubs (3♣) over whatever he rebids. This demands that opener shall pass. The chances that you can use these clubs in no-trumps are hundreds to one against (of course it *could* happen; opener holds ♣A K 3 and two aces!); but your bidding should be based on probabilities – not on miracles.

QUESTION 30

You are sitting East and defending against 4♠ which your partner, West, has doubled. He leads ◇A to your bid suit and South ruffs. Now South crosses to dummy's ♠K and tries to take discards on dummy's diamond honours. What do you discard on ◇K?

North
♠K 4
♡Q 5 3
◇K Q 9 5 4
♣Q 7 3

East
♠5 3
♡K J 2
◇J 10 8 7 6 3 2
♣A

QUESTION 31

Partner deals and bids 1NT (15–17 points). What do you respond on:

♠A Q 10 5   ♡9 5 3   ◇K   ♣K Q 10 8 2

QUESTION 32

You deal and bid 1NT to which partner responds 3♣; what do you rebid on:

♠K 5   ♡A 8 2   ◇A Q 5 3   ♣A 9 7 4

ANSWER 30: The Knave of Diamonds

Why: Because you are extremely anxious for West to lead a heart and not a club. It does not matter giving up a high diamond – North can never re-enter to enjoy the long suit. You know West will be able to ruff the second diamond – that is one trick; you will certainly make ♣A and, if West leads the suit *now*, a heart; you have a good chance of breaking the contract if West has either ♡A or even ♡10 9. The high card demands a lead of the higher-ranking suit, after discounting trumps and the suit led. Only if your heart and club holdings were reversed should you throw ◇2 followed by ◇3. The rule for suit preference is that there must be no ambiguity – and here there cannot be; not only would West be a fool to lead a diamond to dummy's otherwise unreachable winner, but he has no diamond to lead!

ANSWER 31: Three Clubs

Why: Because you have genuine slam hopes with such cards, pro-viding only opener fits (*a*) your clubs or (*b*) your spades. If opener holds, say, four spades to king or king-knave, he will bid them as a cost-nothing effort to find an additional parking-place. This 3♣ bid is a genuine forcing take-out, made in the assurance of game and the hopes of slam. If opener tries three of either red suit, you will rebid 3♠. If neither suit excites opener, you will still end up in 3NT.

ANSWER 32: Four Clubs

Why: Because the first thing the maker of a forcing take-out wants to know is: can you support his suit? Here, with four cards to the ace, you assuredly can. This is the hand facing the responder in Question 31. You will see that 7♣ is an easy make. There is another method of at once confirming clubs and also showing an ace – and that is by bidding 3◇. This, over a force, accepts the slam-try implicit in the force and cue-bids the cheapest possible ace. Partners should decide whether they prefer the direct raise or the implicit raise *via* a cue-bid. With strange partners, always make your bidding direct.

QUESTION 33

You deal and bid 1NT (15–17 points). Partner bids 2♡. What do you rebid on:

     ♠A 9 4   ♡A K J 3   ◇K J 5   ♣J 5 2

QUESTION 34

You deal yourself: ♠A Q 10 6 5
                      ♡K J 8 7 5 2
                      ◇A Q
                      ♣ –

What do you bid?

QUESTION 35

You deal yourself: ♠A K J 6 4
                       ♡A Q J 10 6 3
                      ◇K 4
                      ♣ –

What do you bid?

QUESTION 36

You deal and bid 1♡; partner replies 1♠. What do you rebid on:

    ♠Q 7 2   ♡A Q 8 3   ◇K J 10 6   ♣K 10

ANSWER 33: No Bid

Why: Because partner has said in effect: "I cannot stand no-trumps; I have a long, weak suit of hearts which, with your high cards, ought to gather eight tricks. I have no possible chance of making game." In the face of such instructions, it is unwise to disregard them. Responder has some unbalanced hand like this:

♠J 3   ♡9 8 6 5 4 2   ◊4   ♣10 6 4 3

There is no certainty that he holds ♡Q and you will "run 6 tricks". You have been asked – nay, told – to pass. Do so.

ANSWER 34: One Heart

Why: Because you have no need to falsify your holding by bidding the shorter suit first. You have a full 16-count in top-cards, let alone an extremely powerful distribution and are well worth the "reverse" of bidding spades after hearts. On the other hand, your holdings are so broken that is is not worth making an opening two-bid; unless partner can fit one of your suits, there is very little chance of game.

ANSWER 35: Two Hearts

Why: Unlike the hand in Question 34, here your suits are solid. You do not require very much fit from partner to make the game. A two-bid should be forcing for one round (partner with no matter how bad a hand bids 2NT); and when you reverse with 3♠, he can either bid 4♡, 4◊, or 3NT (which you will take to 4♡). If your two-bid is *not* forcing for one round, you must bid 2♣ on this almost certain game-hand. The trouble with bidding 2♣ on it is that responder, with (say) ♣A Q and either ♡K or ♠Q, is likely to put you into an unmakable slam.

ANSWER 36: One No-trump

Why: The hand counts 15 points with two tens surplus; but it is certainly not worth 2NT. It is not wholly suitable for a spade raise – the trump support is not ideal. The bidding of a second suit (2◊) is not desirable on 4-4-3-2 hands, unless there is absolutely no alternative; and this type of hand, with tenaces, needs to be led up to. If partner is unbalanced, he will bid again; if he is good, he will bid again. You will lose nothing by your conservative rebid of 1NT.

QUESTION 37

You bid 1♣ and partner says 1♡; what do you rebid on:

♠Q J 10 6　　♡Q　　♢A 3　　♣A Q 9 7 5 4

QUESTION 38

You open 1♡ and partner says 2♣; what do you rebid on:

♠J 7　　♡A K J 10 4　　♢A J 5 3　　♣8 2

QUESTION 39

At Game and 60 up, you bid 1♠ and partner replies 1NT. What do you rebid on:

♠A K J 10 9 5　　♡A Q 9 5 3　　♢5　　♣2

ANSWER 37: One Spade

Why: Because it is quite possible for there to be a game in spades, even though, if you rebid your six-card suit, partner could not bid spades at all and would have little ambition to do so. Give responder no more than (say) ace to five hearts and king to four spades – and the 4♠ contract is probably lay-down. If partner cannot raise the spade, you will still be able to play in a part-score in clubs; over his 1NT, you will simply rebid your own long suit – but you must not prematurely resign the hand to a part-score in a minor.

ANSWER 38: Two Diamonds

Why: For two reasons: (*a*) it is possible 2◊ is a make when 2♡ is not, despite the disparity of your two red suits; (*b*) the diamond bid may induce responder to bid no-trumps. In addition, the bidding of the comparatively weak diamond suit does not rule out a heart contract – responder may revert to, or even raise, the red major. When the hand was actually held, responder passed 2◊ almost without thought on:

♠10 5 4   ♡3   ◊10 9 7 6   ♣A Q J 5 4

Declarer scored 40 below and 20 above (worth 130–50 for the part-score) instead of "no score" two down in 2♡ less 100 honours. Honours should seldom influence bidding.

ANSWER 39: Two Spades

Why: With a mere 1NT response, all thoughts of slam must be ruled out. At a love score, you would toss-up mentally between re-bidding 2♡ and 3♡. But with your sole ambition to make the rubber – which, with your present hand is highly probable, you (for once!) *do* allow your honour holding to influence your bidding. You are pretty certain to make eight tricks in either hearts or spades, so you may as well collect the extra hundred for honours. (At match-point duplicate, where honours do not count and there is no part-score you would, of course, show the hearts at whatever level.)

QUESTION 40

You bid 1♠ and partner replies 1NT. What do you rebid on:

♠A Q J 10 8 4   ♡7   ◇6   ♣A Q J 9 6

QUESTION 41

You deal yourself: ♠A Q 4 2
                       ♡A J 7 4
                       ◇A K J 10
                       ♣8

What do you bid?

QUESTION 42

You open 1♡ and partner replies 2♣; what do you rebid on:

♠K Q 7   ♡K Q 9 5 3   ◇K J 4   ♣J 2

ANSWER 40: Three Clubs

Why: Because with a freak of such strength, you should insist upon game. It is, of course, possible to lose four tricks – two red aces and two black kings; it is equally possible that you will make twelve tricks – one red ace in your dummy and one successful finesse (or one black king to four). Of course, you should not anticipate either the fantastic good, or the fantastic bad luck; but bid to averages. It is possible that 5♣ may – just – prove a safer contract than 4♠ (responder may have a singleton spade and four clubs to the king – hence you offer him a choice).

ANSWER 41: One Heart

Why: Because this is the bid most likely to reach the best contract. If you open 1♠ and receive a response of 2♣ or 1NT, you will be wondering what to rebid, hearts or diamonds. If you pick diamonds a possible heart game will go out of the window if responder holds something like ♡Q 9 6 2 in a hand not good enough to bid again; if you pick hearts, you may lose a safe part-score (with 100 honours, partner!) in the red minor. If you open 1◇, you will find it very awkward to rebid over either of the more probable responses; you will reverse, without sufficient length in your first-bid suit. 1♡ gets you out of all trouble; if partner has four respectable spades, he will bid them; if he doesn't bid them, you can rebid diamonds in the certainty you are losing nothing – while if he has four hearts, he will raise you.

ANSWER 42: Two Hearts

Why: Because, although you have a count of 15, which (facing a two-level response) is sometimes considered worth 2NT, yours is not a good hand; you are missing all four aces; you have only a minor fit with partner; and you have no solid suit of your own to run. Only if partner can raise another bid do you want to be in game. If he has 11 or more points, he *will* bid again; if he has only 10, this is one of the "combined 25-point" hands on which you should be glad to be out of game.

QUESTION 43

You reply 1♡ to partner's opening 1◇ bid; he rebids 2♣. What is your second response on:

      ♠A Q 8 4   ♡A Q 8 5 3   ◇J 3 2   ♣6

QUESTION 44

Partner opens 2◇. What do you respond on:

      ♠A Q 8 4   ♡A Q 9 7 5 3   ◇A 8 2   ♣ –

QUESTION 45

Partner opens 1♣; you force with 2♠; partner bids 4♣; what is your next bid on:

           ♠A K Q J 8
           ♡A K Q 3
           ◇A J 10 3
           ♣ –

QUESTION 46

Your partner opens 1◇ and you reply 1♠: your partner rebids 2♡. What should you say next on:

      ♠J 10 9 5 3   ♡A 2   ◇Q J 5 3   ♣9 6

ANSWER 43: Three No-trumps

Why: 2NT is a very weak-sounding bid and should not contain more than 11 points after you have bid a suit; there is no earthly need to bid the fourth suit (spades). If opener has a big minor two-suiter, with one major king, he is quite capable of proceeding – so you will not be missing a slam. Unless you bid 3NT, however, you will be in grave danger of missing a game.

ANSWER 44: Two Hearts

Why: Because, so far as you can see, you are headed certainly for a small slam and probably for a grand slam; and it is essential to employ all bidding space available for constructive exploration. A direct 4NT bid would be idiotic! You know that, opening a two-bid, partner has ♣A – and this is waste paper! Over whatever re-bid partner makes, you will reverse with 3♠; over whatever he bids next, you will bid 6♢. Now, he will know all about it. You may well end in 7NT. The great thing is, when you have the "stuff", DON'T HURRY.

ANSWER 45: Seven Clubs

Why: Because partner has announced a solid club suit with no losers and that means *at least* a six-card suit (not even A K Q J 10 counts as "solid" when you jump in a forcing situation); and you have *no assurance at all* that you can get into his hand to enjoy his clubs! This hand was a feature of a pairs duplicate and most people played in 7NT, losing a heart and two diamonds. But 7♣ was on ice – opener holding:

♠7 2   ♡8 4   ♢9 3   ♣A K Q J 10 9 5

Trust in partner (and adjusting your own bidding to what he shows) is the cardinal requisite of good bridge.

ANSWER 46: Four Diamonds

Why: First of all, without a club guard, no-trumps is "out"; secondly, you cannot rebid spades on so feeble a suit – nor should you want to; thirdly, you cannot raise a secondary suit with only two cards in it. So you are down to putting partner back to diamonds. If you bid only 3♢, however, you are grossly under-bidding your values. By reversing (bidding a higher-ranking suit secondarily) partner is prepared to play in his first suit with no more than a doubleton opposite – and is prepared to play at the three-level. You have a full-fledged diamond raise. Mere "correction" (from 2♡ to 3♢) implies indifference; in order to show your raise, you must jump—not to 3♢ but to 4♢.

QUESTION 47

Your partner opens 1♡; what should you respond on:

♠A 7 2   ♡Q 8   ◇Q J 9 8   ♣Q 9 7 6

QUESTION 48

Here you have a whale of a hand; what do you open on:

♠K Q J 10 9 6   ♡K Q J 10 8   ◇A   ♣A

QUESTION 49

You open 1♣ and partner forces with 2♡; you rebid 3♣ and partner persists with 3♡; you emphasize your single-suited hand with 4♣ and partner now bids 5NT (showing three aces and the king of a bid suit—which you can identify positively as ♡K). What do you bid on:

♠J 3 2   ♡10 5   ◇A 4   ♣K Q J 9 6 2

ANSWER 47: Two Clubs

Why: Because, although you have a scattered 11 points, the hand is unsuitable for a direct 2NT bid; on the other hand, it is too good for 1NT. You might wonder whether 2◇ – in which you have Q J instead of Q 9 – would not be better; it would not because, if partner has four cards in clubs, he will not be able to bid them, in an average opening, over 2◇; while, if he has four cards in diamonds, he *will* be able to bid them over 2♣. If, on the other hand, he has clubs with you, he can raise you and you will not miss a possible club contract. With two four-card suits in response, bid the cheaper first.

ANSWER 48: Four No-trumps

Why: Because the only thing in which you are interested is aces; the two minor-suit king-queens are of no value to you whatever. The conventional opening of 2♣ (unless played with the ace responses) is sure to muddle future bidding. An opening 4NT asks for aces either on the Culbertson principle (naming any ace held – by bidding 5 of the suit; bidding 6♣ to show ♣A and 5♣ to show no ace; and bidding 5NT to show two aces); or on the Blackwood principle, according to partnership arrangement. The 4NT opening bid is never made without two aces – and must be safe for a five contract at its best suit. Only if the announcement of aces as held by partner will enable opener infallibly to determine the final contract should an opening 4NT ever be made.

ANSWER 49: Seven Clubs

Why: Because you can see the probability of thirteen tricks. Partner surely has six hearts – yet he is not solid in hearts or he would have bid *four* no-trumps (not five) to take control of the auction: he also must have more than the four key-cards – and probably holds an extra king. If this is in diamonds, the hand is easy; if in spades, only a singleton ace of clubs will prevent the hand from being (on normal distribution) a spread; you will be able to ruff partner's hearts good for your discards.

QUESTION 50

You force with 2♡ over partner's 1♣ opening; over his 3♣ rebid, you continue with 3♡; when he bids 4♣, you bid 5NT, showing three aces and ♡K. When partner responds 6♡ – an encouraging bid – what is your next effort on:

    ♠A 8 4   ♡A K J 9 7 6 4   ◇K 3   ♣A

QUESTION 51

You hear an opening of 4♠ on your left and partner bids 4NT for a take-out. What do you respond on:

    ♠A   ♡K 9 3 2   ◇Q 8 4 3   ♣J 10 8 6

QUESTION 52

West opens a weak no-trump and East removes this to 2◇; North now comes in with 2♡. When East passes, what do you, South, bid on:

    ♠10 2   ♡9 5 4   ◇A K 8 2   ♣A K 6 3

QUESTION 53

Partner deals and passes; East bids 1♡; what do you, South, bid on:

    ♠Q J 9   ♡A 4   ◇A K Q J 6 3   ♣A K

ANSWER 50: Six No-trumps

Why: Because you do not know whether opener has king-queen-*ten* to six, or king-queen-*knave* to six clubs. You want to test his holding – which may condition the final contract. If you bid 6♠, you are announcing that your extra king, beyond the cards you have pin-pointed by your 5NT bid, lies in spades – by bidding 6NT, you are indicating strongly that it lies in diamonds. This is the counterpart of Question 49 – and shows that, even if opener does not make the clear-cut decision to bid 7♣ direct (as he should) you ought still to reach that goal.

ANSWER 51: Five Spades

Why: Because you are virtually certain of a small slam somewhere and probably a grand slam; partner must be enormous to bid 4NT and the sole question in your mind should be, *not* "can we make it?" but "which suit shall we play in?" Partner probably has a five-card suit – and that is your "spot". If *you* choose, you might strike his three-card suit – and that might be disastrous, for any outstanding length will be on your left.

ANSWER 52: Four Hearts

Why: North must have a reasonable heart suit to come in with a bid even against such weak bidding as East-West's; since you have four solid tricks, there is nothing else for North to hold but something like ace-queen-knave to five or six. You can reckon to lose two spades and one outside minor card (such as the queen of clubs) but no more. A raise to 3♡ is not enough; never ask partner to do something you can do yourself.

ANSWER 53: Three No-trumps

Why: Because, even without a spade lead you are absolutely certain to make nine tricks. You are not interested in hearing of some weak four-card suit from North, so it is pointless to double. It is equally pointless to bid 2♡, since you can support a weak bid neither in spades nor clubs, for you are too short in both suits. It is highly improbable you will make a slam – you must assume East to hold ace-king of spades and king-queen of hearts. This is a case on which to apply the old maxim: "Bid what you think you can make."

QUESTION 54

North opens 1◇ and you, South, reply 1♡; North rebids 2♣ and you properly reply 2♠. If North rebids (*a*) 2NT or (*b*) 3♣, what is your next call on:

    ♠K Q 10 8 2   ♡K J 9 7 4 3   ◇ –   ♣9 4

QUESTION 55

North opens 1♡ and you respond 1♠; North rebids 2◇ and – being rather too good for 3NT, you temporize with 3♣; North jumps to 4♠. What is your next bid on:

    ♠A 10 7 3   ♡10 4   ◇K 10 5   ♣A K 8 6

QUESTION 56

East opens 1♡; what do you, South, bid on:

    ♠A J 7 4   ♡A Q J 3   ◇Q 6 2   ♣10 9

ANSWER 54: Three Spades

Why: Because you are too unbalanced to play in no-trumps and you are too good to resign the hand to 3♣. Your 3♠ bid pin-points your 6–5 distribution – you have bid spades twice, so you have five cards in them; you have bid hearts before spades, so you have more hearts than spades. In the event North held ace to three spades, no hearts and five in each minor headed by ace and ace-king. Knowing that your second suit was five cards long, he could comfortably bid 4♠. Always, when you can, show your precise "shape" – it makes life easy for partner.

ANSWER 55: Five Diamonds

Why: Because there should be a good chance for slam here and this is the most informative bid you can make. You don't know whether North is 4–5–4–0 or 3–5–4–1 or 3–5–5–0 in distribution – one of these he must be. Over 5◇, he can judge precisely what he should do; put you back to spades if he is the first; bid the slam in diamonds if he is the last (and is good enough); and take what action his cards dictate on the middle one. With all these top-cards and no tenaces, a direct 3NT bid over 1♡ is not to be recommended – the point-count value giving place (as it always should) to intelligent application.

ANSWER 56: No Bid

Why: Because any alternative action is likely to lead you into trouble while a pass is likely to lead opponents into trouble. You have a fine opening bid, but you know that your best suit may be stacked against you; if you double, and North replies with the more-than-probable 2♣, you will have to remove to 2♡. No good player wishes to embark on a two-level contract with a four-card suit and a partner marked as weak in high cards. You are, with 14 points, not so good that you can anticipate a game – so pass and be content to defend; if North happens to hold the balance of the cards, you will be delighted to co-operate.

QUESTION 57

You open 1♠ and partner responds with 2◇; you rebid 2♡ and partner produces the fourth suit with 3♣. What do you say on:

♠K Q 10 9 8   ♡A Q 10 9   ◇ –   ♣K J 7 3

QUESTION 58

North opens 2NT. What do you respond on:

♠K 6 5 4   ♡K 8   ◇K Q J 10 6 5   ♣2

QUESTION 59

North opens 1NT (15–17 points) and East (not vulnerable) butts in with 2♣; what do you, South, bid on:

♠A 8 5 3   ♡Q 9 6 4   ◇A 6   ♣5 4 3

QUESTION 60

A protracted bidding sequence is needed before the key bid in this hand. Partner, North, opens 2♠ and you hold:

♠A 7
♡8 4 3
◇A Q 9 7 4
♣10 5 2

You reply 3◇ and, over 3♡ correct to 3♠; partner tries 4♣ and you go to 4♠. North persists with 5♠. Now what do you bid?

ANSWER 57: Four Clubs

Why: Because there is no reason to think that the fourth suit is necessarily non-existent; it should be treated as natural until partner's subsequent bidding makes it clear it has been used merely as a temporizer. If North really has a club suit, that is the place to play; if he has not, he will know what to do in the face of your raise – for he must not make a phoney bid unless he knows what to do if it is raised. Your job is to bid your cards naturally – and a club raise is obvious. You do not jump to *five* clubs because the situation is forcing.

ANSWER 58: Six Diamonds

Why: It would be almost enough to say: "Because you think you will make it." The reasoning is, however, a little more precise than that. For seven to be "on", North must hold *at least* all four aces, spade queen (and preferably knave) and either club king or heart queen; in other words, exact cards. You cannot find out something like the knave of spades or the (useless) club queen. He will not have a superfluity of high cards, or he would have opened 2♣ (with a 2NT rebid; you know he is balanced by his 2NT opener). So you bid what you think you can make.

ANSWER 59: Three No-trumps

Why: Because it is inconceivable that North has no club guard when you hold 10 points with nothing in clubs and he has the average holding of 16 and when not one of your 10 lies in clubs. If East had solid clubs, he would have passed and defeated the no-trumper. The "easy" (or lazy) bid of "Double" should be rigorously eschewed; you may – and in the event you would – be rejecting 600 for a vulnerable game for 300 (or 500 on a double-dummy defence); a poor bargain either at the rubber-bridge table or at match-points.

ANSWER 60: No Bid

Why: With two aces and partner slam-hunting, you refuse to co-operate! Do you see why? Your ◇A is waste-paper! You have no ruffing-values for North and, although he is obviously strong, he has not opened 2♣. You have losers in hearts (and there is no reason to suppose that North's hearts – a genuine suit clearly, since he bid them before knowing where the hand was to be played – are solid); you have *three* losing clubs facing the cue-bid (clearly a cue since a 5–4–4–0 would scarcely be opened with a two-bid). Give yourself a spade more and a club fewer and the doubleton facing a cue-bid would justify the slam since there was a third trump to employ as a ruff. But on the present hand, pass.

QUESTION 61

You open 1♡ and partner responds 1NT. What do you rebid on:

♠A   ♡A K 9 7   ◇A Q 9 8   ♣K 8 5 3

QUESTION 62

North opens 1♣; what do you respond on:

♠J 10 3   ♡10 8 5   ◇7 4   ♣K 7 6 5 2

QUESTION 63

You open 2◇ and North replies 3♣; you rebid 3♡ and North bids 3NT. What action do you take on:

♠2   ♡A K Q 2   ◇A K J 9 8 7   ♣A 8

QUESTION 64

You open 2NT and North bids 3♠. What do you say on:

♠A Q 5   ♡A K   ◇A 10 8 6   ♣A 10 9 3

ANSWER 61: Three Clubs

Why: Because it is clear that opponents hold at least nine spades between them (partner would have bid a four-card spade suit if he had one); therefore, any hope of scrambling nine tricks in no-trumps is unlikely with but a single (and over-quick) stop in spades. On the other hand, you are too good to resign hopes of game – if only you can find a fit. Over 3♣, partner can bid a four-card diamond suit (if he holds one), which he could not bid at the two-level over 1♡. If he raises clubs, you will go to 5♣; if he bids 3◇, you will go to 5◇; if he corrects to 3♡, you can either gamble 4♡ or give him a triple choice by bidding 4◇.

ANSWER 62: Two Clubs

Why: To bid 1NT over 1♣ requires something like a count of 8 or 9 – you have not got it; to bid a different suit requires four cards – you have not got one; to pass allows opponents to come in too easily; if you can possibly avoid doing this, you should. Therefore, your sole resource is to raise the minor opening. You do not know – you cannot – whether North is going to pass 2♣, bid 2NT or even 3NT or just bid 5♣; that is none of your concern at this stage.

ANSWER 63: Four Clubs

Why: Because you need not resign the hand short of slam yet. When North bid 3♣ over 2◇, he must have had a reasonable suit; he would have bid 2NT or 3NT according to his values if he had not. It is clear he has no length in either red suit and not sufficient spades to bid them; so he is probably 3–3–2–5 or 4–2–2–5. In any event, he certainly holds five fair clubs (he must, as he misses ♣A); and you cover all his red losers and have a ruffing value in spades. If opponents lead trumps, he may well be able to set up your diamonds; if they do not, he will set up a spade ruff.

ANSWER 64: Four Clubs

Why: Because you wish to make a slam-try, having the spade fit (responder must have five cards to take out of 2NT) and controls; yet you do not want to go beyond the possible limit of 4♠. You therefore make your try below the game level; and you cue-bid your lowest ace first. Please note that North must not assume from this 4♣ bid that you have bid 2NT on the strength of a long and solid club suit and are running away from spades; the 2NT bid on the long, solid minor is (or should be) seldom called. In any case, even if the opening were made on such cards, the rebid would then be 3NT.

QUESTION 65

Partner opens 2NT and you reply 3♠. Opener rebids 4♣. What do you say on:

    ♠Q 9 8 7 6   ♡Q 9 8   ◊5   ♣K Q 8 4

QUESTION 66

West bids 1◊ and North butts in with 2♣. East passes. What do you, South, do on:

    ♠Q 10 9 8 7 2   ♡Q 8 6   ◊K 8 7 6   ♣ −

QUESTION 67

You, South, open 1♠; West butts in with 2♣; North bids 2♡. What do you rebid on:

    ♠K Q 9 8 7   ♡J 2   ◊A Q 6 4 2   ♣2

QUESTION 68

You open 1♡ and partner bids 2NT; what do you rebid on:

    ♠A K Q   ♡Q 10 9 7 6   ◊J 10 9 4 2   ♣ −

ANSWER 65: Five Clubs

Why: What else should you bid? This shows either ♣K or support; it may, as here, show both. The primary purpose of this 5♣ bid, however, is not only to show K and/or four cards in clubs but to accept the slam-try. One thing is certain; after the acceptance with 5♣, partner is not going to pass; if he cue-bids a red suit, you will transfer to 6♠; if he chooses to slam in clubs (having four himself and believing that the 4–4 club fit is likely to be better than the 5–4 or 5–3 spade fit), you will accept his judgement.

ANSWER 66: No Bid

Why: Because a good bridge axiom is: do not squeal unless you are hurt; in other words, do not run (and not always then) unless you are doubled. If you voluntarily rescue into 2♠, North may easily go 3♣; then you may be doubled. You need not, at this moment, take premature action. If West doubles and East leaves the double in, then – and only then – should you bid 2♠. (Conceivably, if West now produces two of a red suit, you might contest with 2♠). On a weak hand, the thing to do is to pass if you are in no peril of a serious penalty.

ANSWER 67: Two Spades

Why: Because you are not good enough to push the bidding to the three-level. Only if North takes further action should you show the diamonds – over, say, 2NT, or a cue-bid of 3♣. You opened 1♠ because you anticipated (on the basis of probabilities) that North would reply 2♣; this gave you an easy rebid of 2◊. When, however, the course of the auction precludes this low and easy rebid, you have to suppress the diamond suit and content yourself with a simple repeat of your five-card major.

ANSWER 68: Three Diamonds

Why: Your only reason for opening was because you had two five-card suits; there is no reason to suppress them. A contract of 3♡ or 4◊ (both of which you will pass) is preferable to one of 2NT. If responder jumps to 4♡, you have every reason to hope to make it. You certainly have more chance of making nine or ten tricks in a red suit than your partner has of making eight tricks in no-trumps. To rebid 3♡ is injudicious because diamonds may easily prove superior to hearts as a trump suit. Note: the rebid in diamonds promises no more than a rebid in hearts, so far as top-cards go.

QUESTION 69

Partner opens 2NT; you take out to 3♠; partner rebids 3NT. What action do you take on:

      ♠J 9 7 6 4 2   ♡J 9 6 4 2   ◇6   ♣3

QUESTION 70

You open 1♡ and partner responds 1♠; you properly rebid 2NT and partner bids 3◇. What is your next bid on:

      ♠A 7 3   ♡A K J 4   ◇K 8 3   ♣K 10 2

QUESTION 71

You are in luck and deal yourself a 24-point hand; you open 2♣ and, to your surprise, partner makes the positive reply of 2NT. What do you rebid on:

      ♠A K 3   ♡A Q 4   ◇A K J 10   ♣K 10 9

QUESTION 72

You find yourself in the happy position of being able to give a positive response to partner's 2♣ opening. Over your 2NT, he bids 3NT. What do you say next on:

      ♠10 8 7   ♡K 9 3 2   ◇8 3   ♣A 8 6 5

ANSWER 69: Four Hearts

Why: Because your hand is certain to develop tricks in one of your spidery suits and is valueless in no-trumps. Opener should not get excited on your bidding but merely pass 4♡ or put you back to 4♠ as his cards dictate. To rebid 4♠ would be better than passing 3NT, but would forgo the chance of playing in a comfortable 4♡ if partner held (say) ♠K 3 and ♡A Q 7 3. If you were really good, you would not make so *piano* a bid as 4♡; you would bid 5♡; so partner, hearing only 4♡, should not expect much from you except shape (which you have).

ANSWER 70: Three Spades

Why: You do not know whether partner is good or bad; the only things you do know are: that he cannot support hearts and he does not like no-trumps. To rebid 3NT is tantamount to insulting your partner. It is also inviting a club lead (where you have but one slender guard) and committing yourself to galloping off nine tricks without losing the lead. There are plenty of hands partner can hold where 4♠ is on ice and 3NT is out of the window – and also plenty of hands where he can make 3♠ but you cannot make 2NT. If he passes 3♠, it may be sad but it will probably be more profitable than going down.

ANSWER 71: Three No-trumps

Why: You are, believe it or not, minimum for your bid and should, in consequence, make a minimal response. Partner has announced an ace and a king *and no shape* – that means, no length which your top cards can establish. It is equally pointless either to bid 3◇ (you have little chance of making 5◇) or 4NT (which is not conventional but quantitative). If partner has more than his ace and king – if, say, he has a count of 10–11, he will make an effort and you will gladly accept it. As yet, he has but 7 points to add to your 24 – and a combined 31 with no long suit does not augur well for a slam.

ANSWER 72: No Bid

Why: You have said your piece with your first (positive) reply. It is, therefore, merely bidding to a loss to make some experimental effort such as 4♣, 4♡ or 4NT. This one is responder to the previous hand. Even if you get the diamond finesses right, you will make only two spades, three hearts, four diamonds and two clubs; eleven tricks. It would be too much to hope that they will establish a club finesse for you *and* that the diamonds will prove worth four tricks.

QUESTION 73

Partner opens 2♣ and you reply 2NT. Partner bids 3NT. What do you say on:

♠Q 4 2   ♡K J 6 3   ◊Q 5 4   ♣A 8 3

QUESTION 74

You are still holding good cards. What do you open on:

♠A K Q J 9 8 5 4 3   ♡ –   ◊A K Q   ♣6

QUESTION 75

Still in the vein, you force with 2♠ over partner's opening bid of 1♡. Partner now bids 4♡. Very annoying – or is it? What is your next bid on:

♠A K J 4 2   ♡ –   ◊A K J 7   ♣A K Q 3

ANSWER 73: Six No-trumps

Why: Because you can count a minimum of 35 points – which should be enough for twelve tricks even without a five-card suit (which you may assume the partnership does not possess). Partner should have 23–24 and you hold 12; that brings you to 35–36 – but does not bring you to 37–38 which are needed for the grand slam. If partner has something like 26 points, he will be quite capable of continuing. In other words, if you had responded 2♦ (negative) and he was going to bid only 2NT he will pass your 6NT; if he was good enough to jump 3NT on his own over a negative, he will go to 7NT once he knows you can guarantee 6NT; he will have values to spare.

ANSWER 74: Four No-trumps

Why: Because this is the only bid which will at once enable you to compel partner to give you the specific information you require and to limit your final contract in the light of his reply. Partner's duty is to disclose his aces (if any). If he has no aces he bids 5♣; if he has the ♣A he bids 6♣. This enables partner to bid the grand slam in spades. If, however, the responder has the ♡A, he bids 5♡; in this instance partner realizing he has a club loser settles for 6♠.

ANSWER 75: Seven hearts

Why: Because opener's jump rebid *in a forcing situation* has no possible justification other than to inform you that he has a long *and dead solid* suit. It must be six cards long (and, if only so long as that, must be headed by ♡A K Q J at least; no mere five-card suit; even all five honours is not enough to justify the jump rebid). Therefore, your seven certain winners added to his advertised six sure winners counts up to thirteen tricks; bid it! But – *do not bid it in no-trumps*; with no heart in your own hand, you have no assurance that partner will ever be able to get in! With A K Q J to six or better, he does not need an extra queen either to open or to make this jump.

QUESTION 76

Partner opens 2♡. What do you respond on:

    ♠A K Q J 8 7 3   ♡4 3 2   ◇7 6   ♣9

QUESTION 77

You open 1♠ and partner responds 3♠. What do you say next on:

    ♠A K 9 3   ♡Q J 10 2   ◇K 5 4   ♣10 7

QUESTION 78

Partner opens 2♣. What do you respond on:

    ♠K J 3 2   ♡K 8 4   ◇5 3   ♣Q J 8 7

QUESTION 79

Partner opens 1♠; you hold a fairly balanced 11-point hand; what do you respond on:

    ♠Q 2   ♡10 7 5   ◇A J 10 6   ♣K J 7 2

ANSWER 76: Three Spades

Why: An opening bid of two is a (one-round) forcing-bid. You jump in a forcing situation for only one reason: to show an absolutely solid suit of your own. This you possess, and the information must be communicated to partner without delay. Unless he can be assured that your spades are of this quality, he can never be certain how high to go; even with three aces (and his promised good heart suit) he will always fear a spade loser.

ANSWER 77: No Bid

Why: Because the double-raise of an opening bid is *not* a game-force but a limit-bid, announcing that responder can see a fair chance of making nine tricks with spades as trumps. If responder thought there were a reasonable chance of making ten tricks, he would (*a*) have bid 4 direct; or (*b*) bid a different suit preparatory to giving a delayed game raise. It is losing tactics to bid to what you can see is a certain loss: what hope have you, on these cards, of making ten tricks with only a double-raise opposite? Pass – and hope you make your contract!

ANSWER 78: Four Spades

Why: Because this is a specialized bid, devised expressly for this type of hand: viz., good trump support; fair values; *but no ace or void.* It informs opener marked with a good hand worth eight or more playing tricks, that he must hold at least *three* first-round controls in his own hand before he can even think of slams. At the same time, it assures him that his trump suit is well supported. If opener held

♠Q 10 9 8 7 6 5   ♡A   ◇A K 3   ♣A 2

(or something equivalent) he might well choose to go direct to 6♠ in comfort.

ANSWER 79: Two Clubs

Why: Proceed by the method of elimination. First, you cannot raise spades with only a doubleton; secondly, you cannot bid no-trumps properly with the hearts unguarded; thirdly, you are, therefore, down to bidding a minor suit. Although the diamonds are a point stronger, bidding them may cut out a club contract – it is unlikely that partner will be good enough to bid *three* clubs over two diamonds. If partner rebids spades, you might (assured of length in his hand) bid 3♠; if he bids 2♡, you can then try 2NT. The rule is: respond with the lower-ranking of four-card suits . . . providing the suit be reasonable.

QUESTION 80

Partner opens 1♠; what do you respond on:

♠Q 2   ♡10 8   ◇10 9 8 7 3   ♣A K Q 3

QUESTION 81

Partner opens 1♠; you properly respond 2♣, bidding the lower of biddable four-card suits; partner rebids 2♠; what do you say next on:

♠4 3 2   ♡10 7   ◇A Q J 4   ♣A K 10 6

QUESTION 82

You opened 1♠ and, over partner's bid of 2◇, correctly repeated 2♠. Over partner's next bid – 3♣, you corrected, again properly, to 3◇. Partner's third bid is 4♠. What do you say next on:

♠A K J 10 5   ♡8 6 5 3   ◇K 4 2   ♣Q

ANSWER 80: Two Diamonds

Why: Because your diamonds, though weaker than your clubs, are a *five-* (instead of a *four-*) card suit. If opener rebids 2♠, you will give him 2NT in the almost certainty that clubs will be led; if diamonds are raised, you will try 3♣; if spades are rebid, you will push on to 3♠. There is little danger that bidding the diamonds will cause a loss because partner leads your topless suit; with 11 points facing an opening bid, you do not expect to defend; and if fourth-hand bids 2♡ and this is passed round to you, you can contest the part-score with either 3♣ (best) or 2♠.

ANSWER 81: Four Spades

Why: Because there is no earthly point in either chancing no-trumps (with the risk of losing five heart tricks off the reel); or of bidding 3◇. To bid 3◇ does not *primarily* ask opener to bid no-trumps if he has a heart guard; its cardinal purpose is to ask for preference to clubs – if possible at the five level. Suppose you *do* bid 3◇ at this point and partner goes 5♣ – you may easily fail at an eleven-trick contract; while, if you revert to spades, partner will surely read you for a singleton heart and may

    (on   ♠A K Q J 7   ♡8 7 5   ◇K 7 2   ♣Q 2)

contract for a slam which – *if* your bidding had been accurate – would have been on ice; but which, in fact, will infallibly lose two hearts at once.

ANSWER 82: Six Spades

Why: Because partner is marked, for a certainty, with a singleton heart; your king of diamonds and queen of clubs should convince you that you will not only lose nothing in the minor suits but also should obtain some discards of your losing hearts on dummy's high cards. There can be no immediate risk of losing two hearts; and partner's jump in spades sounds very much as if he held ♠Q. The slam should be lay-down – as it was, responder holding:

    ♠Q 4 2   ♡7 ◇A Q 6 5 3   ♣A J 9 8

Only if diamonds do not divide 3–2 (66 per cent) will the slam depend on the club finesse or being able to ruff 2 hearts.

QUESTION 83

You open 1♠ and partner responds 2◇; you rebid 2♠ and partner bids 3♣; you correct to 3◇ and partner next bursts into 4♠. What do you say next on:

♠A K Q 10 6;   ♡K J 4   ◇8 7 3   ♣J 7

QUESTION 84

You deal yourself an awkward hand. What do you open on:

♠A K Q 10   ♡K J 3   ◇8 7 4   ♣7 5 3

QUESTION 85

You bid 1♠ and partner replies 2◇, or, perhaps 2♣. What do you rebid on:

♠A K Q 10   ♡K J 3   ◇8 7 4   ♣7 5 3

ANSWER 83: No Bid

Why: Because your king of hearts, facing a marked singleton opposite, is of little or no value – it is what is termed "duplication". Moreover, there is no reason to think that your knave of clubs is sufficient to ensure running dummy's minor suits without loss. The whole art of bidding is not only to describe your own hand correctly, but to infer from partner's bidding which of your values is pulling its weight – here, four of your 14 points you can throw out of the window, and another one (♣J) being in responder's second suit, is not really very effective.

ANSWER 84: One Spade

Why: What are your alternative choices? You certainly cannot afford to pass with a full third of the high cards in the pack; to bid 1♣ on such a hand distorts it out of all recognition; to bid 1NT falsifies its high-card count (if you are playing a "strong no-trump") and falsifies its high-card location even if you are playing the "weak no-trump" – a no-trumper should be guarded in three, not two, suits and should *not* have the bulk of its power in a major. Yes – I know there is a difficulty; but a subsequent problem will show you how to solve it.

ANSWER 85: Two Spades (!)

Why: Because it is the only sensible bid available to you! You certainly cannot raise partner's take-out; nor can you, on a mere 13-count, rebid 2NT (which, even over a take-out at the two-level, must postulate about 15–16 points). Now, what is the danger of rebidding this four-card suit? First, that partner, banking on length, may raise you sky-high in spades on, perhaps, no more than a doubleton knave. If partner does this, you will still have a very good chance of making your contract, for your spades are solid and you can draw four rounds, before making partner's high cards. You would think little shame to rebid 2♠ on, say, ♠K Q 7 4 2; well, here high cards compensate for length (just as, conversely, length may sometimes compensate for high cards).

QUESTION 86

You bid 1♠ and partner responds 2♡; what should you rebid on:

      ♠A K Q 10   ♡K J 3   ◇8 7 4   ♣7 5 3

QUESTION 87

Partner makes the startling opening bid of 5♠. What do you respond on:

     ♠A 6 4 3 2   ♡8 5 2   ◇8 6   ♣5 4 2

QUESTION 88

West opens 1♣ and, after a pass from your partner, North, East bids 1NT. You double and two more passes allow East to come in again, converting to 2♣. What do you bid on:

    ♠K Q J 7 5   ♡A K Q 9   ◇K J 3   ♣2

ANSWER 86: Three Hearts

Why: Because it is very unlikely that responder will bid *hearts* at the two-level without a five-card suit. Minor suits of four-card length are freely so bid, exploratorily; so are majors at the one-level. Spades can always be bid at the one-level in response; but hearts over spades almost always involve a five-card suit – especially when opener can see from his own hand that the hearts can be at best no better than ♡A Q 10 9. There is no earthly need to rebid your four-card suit on this occasion.

ANSWER 87: Seven Spades (!!!)

Why: Because you have about a 99·99 per cent chance of making it The opening bid of 5♠ (instead of beginning with, say, 2♠ or 2♣) is reserved for a very special type of hand; a hand with losers *only* in the trump suit. It is clear that opener cannot miss more than two high honours (the ace which you hold and either king or queen), or he could not guarantee eleven tricks. Therefore he must have considerable length, plus absolute winners outside – aces, kings or voids. It is inconceivable he has fewer than seven spades. With your five, he can have no spade loser – and you *know* he has nothing else he can lose.

ANSWER 88: Three Clubs (!!!)

Why: Because (*a*) you still have an enormous hand – but one little suited to defending against clubs; and (*b*) North is marked with some values, since he *passed* the double of 1NT. No bid other than this cue-bid of 3♣ can possibly inform North that his bits and pieces are of inestimable value; a bid of 2♠ or 3♠ or of 2♡ (you dare not bid 3♡) will simply look as if you are contesting a part-score, whereas, in fact, you are really insisting upon game. If North bids 3◇, you (having forced to game) can bid 3♠; and, subsequently, over 4◇ (if bid) either bid 4♡ or raise to 5◇.

QUESTION 89

You open 1♡ and West, next to speak, butts in with 1♠; partner
North doubles (for penalties) and East intervenes with 4◊. What
do you say next on:

      ♠K J 6 3   ♡A J 10 9 6 4   ◊ –   ♣K J 2

QUESTION 90

Your partner opens 1♠. What do you respond on:

      ♠K J 7 5 2   ♡10 8 6 4 2   ◊A K   ♣A

QUESTION 91

You open 1♠ and partner forces with 3◊; you, naturally, raise to
4◊. Partner now bids 5♣; what is your next bid on:

      ♠A Q 5 4 3   ♡ –   ◊Q J 5 3   ♣K Q 10 6

ANSWER 89: Four Spades (!!!)

Why: Because it is clear that West's spade bid is psychic when North can make a business double of the intervention at the one-level and you hold king-knave to four; there are, after all, no more than thirteen spades in the pack! It is also pretty clear that North has little or no heart support – or he would not have doubled the spades so quickly. A pass of 4◊ ("they hadn't bid game, partner") is too cowardly to merit consideration.

ANSWER 90: Three Diamonds—NOT Three Hearts

Why: Because you want to show where your tricks actually lie; if you force in hearts, partner will look at queen to three or knave to three as a good fit; he will regard a void in your announced strong suit as a liability. But hearts are not your strong suit at all; and a void is the best thing partner could have. This is one of the occasions when – being able to revert to his higher-ranking suit – you force on top-cards instead of valueless length.

ANSWER 91: Five Hearts

Why: Because 5♣ is a cue-bid and you hold first-round control in hearts. Responder cannot mistake this bid; if you had a two-suiter in the majors, you would have bid 3♡ over 3◊. This is the hand held opposite that above. A 7♠ contract is certain, except in the unlikely event of a first-round ruff. You will reach it if you cue-bid hearts on your void – you will miss it if you don't. Similarly, you will reach it if partner forces in a minor suit but you will miss it if he forces in hearts. Over 5♡ he will bid 5♠; you will now go to 6♣, showing the king and announcing hopes of a grand slam – which he should bid without further ado.

QUESTION 92

Your partner opens 1NT (16–18) and you properly bid 3♠; when opener rebids 3NT, what is your next bid on:

      ♠ A K Q 7 3   ♡8 2   ◇A K 9 4   ♣6 3

QUESTION 93

Partner opens 1♠ third-hand; what do you respond on:

    ♠K 10   ♡K 6   ◇Q 8 6 5 3   ♣K 8 6 4

QUESTION 94

Opponents' bidding has proceeded without interrruption:

South	North
1♠	2♣
2NT	3♠
4♠	

What is your lead from:

    ♠J 6   ♡A K 4   ◇Q J 10 5   ♣J 8 6 2

ANSWER 92: Four Diamonds

Why: Because you are (or should be) absolutely certain of a small slam and you may be able to make a grand slam in diamonds. Since you have two ace-kings, it is almost certain that opener has two aces; and since you have long spades, it may well be possible to make thirteen tricks in diamonds (if partner has four of them) when there are only twelve available in no-trumps. Four no-trumps is not recommended here; authorities are divided on the question of whether the bid is conventional (Blackwood or Culbertson) or quantitative. If you are going to bid no-trumps at all, the only sensible bid is 6NT; with a count of 16 yourself plus a five-card suit which is surely going to run (opener will probably hold ♠J), you are virtually certain to make twelve tricks.

ANSWER 93: Two Diamonds—NOT Two No-trumps

Why: Because, although your kings look as if you would like the lead up to your hand; and although, with a count of 11, you want to excite partner after you have passed, a bid of 2NT should not be made on a 5–4–2–2 distribution. If opener cannot proceed over 2♦, you are likely to miss nothing; game will not be on. Your cards have not improved because you have passed. The key to this hand's success lies in the answer to the question: is partner good or bad? If good, he will continue the bidding; if bad, you do not want to be higher than the two-level.

ANSWER 94: The Queen of Diamonds—NOT the King of Hearts

Why: Because it is essential to establish a trick in diamonds (if one is available) before your top hearts are knocked out. If you lead ♡K (or A according to your methods) and switch to ◇Q, you have lost a tempo; declarer may be able to knock out your other heart honour, win the second diamond, and discard a diamond loser on ♡Q. If you lead ◇Q, you will set up ◇10 before South can establish ♡Q. With your club holding, it is improbable that declarer can shed a heart loser on dummy's suit immediately.

QUESTION 95

Opponents have bid:

	South	North
	1♠	2♣
	2◇	3♠
	4♠	

What is your lead from:

♠K 9 3   ♡Q 8 5 2   ◇A J 3   ♣Q 7 4

QUESTION 96

What do you bid on this hand:

♠Q 10 9 6 4 3 2   ♡A K 10 4   ◇ –   ♣8 5

QUESTION 97

What do you bid on:

♠10 9 5 3   ♡6 2   ◇A K Q J 8 6 3   ♣ –

QUESTION 98

Your partner opens a heart; your right-hand opponent bids a spade; what do you bid on:

♠J 9 4 3 2   ♡J   ◇6 3   ♣A K Q J 10

ANSWER 95: The Three of Spades

Why: Because it looks as if there were some ruffing available in dummy, who is marked with only three trumps, and a possible shortage in diamonds. You should reckon on making ♠K, two diamonds and, perhaps, a trick in partner's hand. The best attack is to cut down a possible cross-ruff; the lead also runs no risk of giving declarer an extra heart trick, should he hold ♡K J.

ANSWER 96: One Spade—NOT Three Spades

Why: It is a very sound rule never to pre-empt in one major suit when holding values in the other. It is better to pass than to bid three spades; but better to bid one spade than to pass. You have, it is true, only a count of nine; but you have two defensive tricks – essential for an opening bid; you have a conventional rebid; and, with both major suits, plus your seven-card length, there is every reason to open in any position. When this hand was actually dealt, the player opened three spades ("only nine points") and went down two, vulnerable – responder held:

♠J   ♡Q J 5 3 2   ◇8 7 6 5   ♣K 10 5

– and a heart contract was sure to make a plus score.

ANSWER 97: One Diamond—NOT Three Diamonds

Why: Because your hand is too good, despite its low point-count, for pre-emption – and to pre-empt fourth-hand is ill-advised. If your passing partner has no more than two aces and a king, you may easily make 3NT . . . but he will not bid it over 3◇. Moreover, why cut out a possible spade contract? Partner may easily hold something like five or six spades and king of hearts. Substitute ◇10 for ◇A or ◇K, and the hand is a pre-emptive opening.

ANSWER 98: Double

Why: Because (*a*) you have no fit with partner; (*b*) by bidding 2♣ you may compel opener to rebid hearts which will not suit you at all; (*c*) if you burst into 2NT or 3NT, opener may take you out in hearts – which again does not augur well. The double is pretty certain to register a plus-score for you; and any other bid holds the potentiality of loss. Only if opener takes out the double should you essay no-trumps – and then only if he takes it out in diamonds; if he takes out the double with 2♡, your correct move is to bid 3♣, in the hope that *he* guards diamonds sufficiently to bid no-trumps.

QUESTION 99

Your partner opens 1NT (16–18 points); what do you respond on:

♠7   ♡8 4 2   ◊10 8   ♣A J 9 7 5 3 2

QUESTION 100

East opens 1♡ and you, South, bid 1♠; your partner, North, bids 1NT. What do you say next on:

♠A K Q 8 4 2   ♡2   ◊Q 7 3   ♣A 8 2

QUESTION 101

You are not vulnerable and opponents are; partner opens 1♡ and the next hand doubles; what do you bid on:

♠ –   ♡10 9 7 6 4 2   ◊J 10 9 8 6 3   ♣5

ANSWER 99: Three No-trumps

Why: The simple answer is this: because you hope to make it! It is true that, with only five points, you may hold a combined total of only 21 – and the average assumption for game is 25–26; but your hand is extremely likely to make seven tricks; opener will hold *either* three clubs *or*, at worst, a doubleton honour, possibly ♣K Q bare. In any event, the odds are on his being able to run the suit. If you can run a seven-card suit, it does not take very much more to amass a total of nine tricks. The odds favour a bid of 3NT.

ANSWER 100: Three No-trumps

Why: Again the simple answer is: because you think you will make it. Partner's 1NT is constructive in this position and assures a very good guard in the adversely-bid hearts; he is not bidding on a single-ton spade and four hearts to the queen with nothing outside! You have the probability of 7½ tricks for his no-trumps – and he should surely produce 1½. What, you may ask yourself, if the spades do not prove to run without loss? The 1NT in the teeth of an opening bid postulates a double-guard; so partner will be able to give up a spade and make five spades only, two hearts and possibly two clubs or two diamonds or one in each minor suit.

ANSWER 101: Five (or six) Hearts

Why: Because it is probable that opponents have the balance of power and it is therefore essential to make them guess at the highest possible level, preventing them from exploring. Do not be misled by your point-count of one – you hold as good as ♠A K Q and ♣K Q. This is a two-way bid; conceivably you may bulldoze opponents into letting you play 5♡ or 6♡ undoubled; conceivably you may even make the contract; conceivably, you may push them into the wrong slam! In the event, one pair of opponents bid 6◊ over 5♡ – which, let me hasten to say, your hand did NOT double; at another table, they doubled 6♡ which were made – with 6♠ on for them.

QUESTION 102

You open 2NT and partner bids a conventional 3♣ – asking you to show your four-card suits in ascending order. What do you rebid on:

♠A K J   ♡A Q 4   ◇Q J 6   ♣A J 8 7

QUESTION 103

Partner opens 2NT and you respond 3♣, asking him to show his four-card suits in ascending order. He replies 3 NT. What is your next bid on:

♠8 5   ♡A 8 5 3   ◇K 7 5   ♣K J 8 6

QUESTION 104

Partner opens 3NT. What do you bid on:

♠K 9 8 7 6 3   ♡K J 8 4 2   ◇8   ♣10

ANSWER 102: Three No-trumps

Why: Because you have no other four-card suit than clubs – and by rebidding 3NT, you show this. If you bid 4♣ and this did not "fit" responder's hand, you would already have passed the 3NT level in which – failing such a fit – he might have regarded as his limit. Give yourself a heart fewer and a diamond more, and you would be prepared to respond 3◇ before either showing, or suppressing, the clubs. You would show the clubs if responder bid 3♠ and suppress them if responder showed 3♡. Thus you get the best of all possible worlds.

ANSWER 103: Six Clubs

Why: Because you know opener has a four-card club suit with you and, also, that he has no four-card heart suit; if he had, he would have shown it, before showing his club holding by bidding 3NT. It is ONLY when he has no four-card suit other than clubs that he will rebid 3NT. With an ace and two kings facing a 2NT opening bid, you should be properly sure of slam once the fit has been found. It is pointless to bid 4NT (Blackwood) because a mere count of points will show you that seven is not a reasonable proposition. Once you know the height at which you are prepared to play *on the combined hands* and the denomination in which you intend to play, determine the contract yourself.

ANSWER 104: No Bid

Why: Because 3NT as an opening bid is a specialized bid which does not show a powerhouse of balanced distribution. Such a hand is better opened 2♣ and rebid either 2NT or 3NT according to its value: 2NT on 23–24 and 3NT on 25 or more. Opener has a long and solid minor with guards here and there; something like

♠Q 3   ♡Q 9   ◇A Q   ♣A K Q J 9 5 2

He will be very distressed to be taken out of a certain three no-trumper into a dubious 4♠.

QUESTION 105

The player on your right deals and bids 1♡; you properly make a take-out double and, over a pass, partner bids (what you least wanted to hear) 1NT; opener contests with 2◊. What do you bid on:

♠A K J 9   ♡7   ◊Q 10 8 6 3   ♣K 10 9

QUESTION 106

You respond 2♡ to partner's opening bid of 1♠; he raises you to 3♡. What do you say next on:

♠Q J 6   ♡K Q 10 8 2   ◊9   ♣A 10 8 6

QUESTION 107

You open the bidding with 1♡ and partner replies 2♣; you rebid 2♡ and partner raises to 4♡. What do you bid next on:

♠A Q J 5   ♡Q 10 9 7 5   ◊A 10 7   ♣3

ANSWER 105: No Bid

Why: Because you should look ahead a little. Supposing you double 2◇; it is virtually certain a correction will come from your left to 2♡. Your double of diamonds will be construed by partner, not necessarily as showing five to the queen, but as showing tops as well as length – and this may easily induce him to double hearts. You will, you see, have bid your cards twice over; the initial take-out double did full justice to your hand – anything else should come from partner. If he doubles 2♡ on his own, you can comfortably accept his judgement; you should not induce him to double by premature action (by doubling 2◇).

ANSWER 106: Four Clubs

Why: Because this is at once the cheapest, the most informative, and the safest slam-try you can make – and the hand is worth slam exploration. If you bid 3♣ and partner goes to 4♣, to show clubs will take you to the five-level. If you bid 4NT (Blackwood) you are at the five-level anyway. On the other hand, if you merely bid 4♡, you may easily miss a lay-down slam. The bid of 4♣ caters for every possibility; opener with a poor hand will simply bid 4♡. If he is a little better and holds ◇A, he can show this cheaply by bidding 4◇. If *he* is excited by your 4♣ bid, he can bid 4NT or make any other bid he chooses.

ANSWER 107: No Bid

Why: Because there is no reason to suppose you can make more than ten tricks! Responder need not be better than three hearts to the knave; quite enough to support a rebid suit. He need not hold ♣A. If responder were concealing gigantic heart support, plus a big club suit, he might well have forced at once. Any slam-try – 4♣ or 5◇ – may well incite responder to proceed too far. This is not a good hand and partner's bidding has made it no better. Had responder replied 2◇ instead of 2♣, you might well hope for big things – but then you would not have rebid 2♡!

QUESTION 108

Dealer, on your left, opens 1♡; partner doubles; opponent on your right bounces to 3♡; what do you bid on:

♠K J 10 6   ♡5   ◇K J 9 6 4 2   ♣7 3

QUESTION 109

Your partner opened 1♣ and you responded 2◇; over 2♡ what is your next bid on:

♠K 3   ♡K J 4   ◇K Q 10 9 5   ♣A J 8

QUESTION 110

Partner opens 1NT (16–18) and you say, properly enough, 3♠; partner rebids 3NT; what do you say now on:

♠A K Q 4 2   ♡8 3   ◇A K 9 3   ♣9 5

ANSWER 108: Four Spades—NOT Five Diamonds

Why: Because (*a*) with a take-out double opposite, you are good enough to expect to make a game; (*b*) because your hand may easily be worth ten tricks but not eleven; (*c*) because the doubler of one major suit is sure to have more-than-adequate support for the other – or he has not a proper double. Not surprisingly, all three conditions were fulfilled in practice – doubler holding

♠A Q 9 7   ♡8 5   ◇A 10 7   ♣K J 10 4

On a heart lead and continuation, you ruffed, drew two rounds of trumps and played on diamonds, playing king and then small, finessing ◇10 if ◇Q did not drop, to protect dummy's clubs. You won the third spade in hand and ran the diamonds, discarding clubs from dummy. Note 5◇ depends on guessing not only ◇Q but also the club position.

ANSWER 109: Two No-trumps

Why: Having forced, there is no risk of being dropped short of game – so there is no need to pre-judge the issue. What is of cardinal importance is that you should make the no-trump bid early in case the final contract should be in no-trumps and your ♠K should be protected from immediate attack. If partner holds ♠A or ♠Q, it will make no difference; if he holds neither, the difference may be stupendous. Opener actually held two small spades, ace-queen to four hearts, ace-knave bare of diamonds and five clubs to king-queen; over 2NT, he bid 3♣; over 3♡ from you he bid 4◇. Now, you can bid 6NT with assurance.

ANSWER 110: Four Diamonds

Why: Because, with a count of 16 plus a surely "working" five-card suit, you are not giving up short of a slam; since opener has no spade support, he may well hold four cards in diamonds. If this is so, you may well make 7◇ where only 6NT is on. Over 4◇, he will check for aces and kings and (if he holds two ace-kings plus queen to four diamonds) will bid the grand slam.

QUESTION 111

Partner bids 1NT (16–18) and you respond 3♠; partner rebids 3NT. What is your next bid on:

♠A K Q 4 2   ♡8 3 2   ◇A K 6   ♣9 5

QUESTION 112

Partner opens 2NT. What do you bid on:

♠K 7 2   ♡Q 6 3   ◇J 8 4   ♣A 6 5 3

QUESTION 113

Partner opens 2NT. What do you respond on:

♠A K Q 3   ♡K 8 4 2   ◇J 3   ♣Q 8 6